P9-CSF-697

— THE —
APPLE
COOKBOOK

BASIC INGREDIENTS

THE
APPLE
COOKBOOK

MORE THAN SIXTY
EASY, IMAGINATIVE RECIPES

EDITED BY
NICOLA HILL

COURAGE
BOOKS
AN IMPRINT OF
RUNNING PRESS BOOK PUBLISHERS

Philadelphia • London

Canadian representatives:
General Publishing Co., Ltd.,
30 Lesmill Road, Don Mills, Ontario M3B 2T6.

10 9 8 7 6 5 4 3 2 1
Digit on the right indicates the number of this printing.
Library of Congress Cataloguing in Publication Number 94-67590

ISBN 1-56138-494-1
Printed in Singapore

Acknowledgements
Commissioning Editor: Nicola Hill
Editors: Isobel Holland & Jo Lethaby
U.S. Consultant: Jenni Fleetwood
Art Editors: Meryl James & Sue Michniewicz
Production Controller: Sasha Judelson
Photographer: Nick Carman
Home Economist: Jennie Shapter
Stylist: Jane McLeish
Illustrator: Marc Adams
Varieties text written by Joan Morgan

This edition published in the United States of America in 1995
by Courage Books
an imprint of Running Press Book Publishers
125 South Twenty-Second Street
Philadelphia, PA 19103-4399

Notes
Microwave methods are based on microwave ovens
with a High Power output of 800 watts.

All the jellies, jams and preserves should be processed in a boiling
water-bath canner according to the U.S.D.A. guidelines.

To core an apple, use an apple corer if keeping the apple whole.
Alternatively, quarter the apple and remove the core with a small
sharp knife. The apple peel can be removed if you like.

CONTENTS

Variety notes – includes appearance to give a general guide to its identity; texture and flavor; and, when appropriate, cooking properties.

Storage – At home, apples should be stored in cool, dark conditions. Centrally heated rooms or warm kitchens are not good places to keep fruit. Fruit that you want to store for any length of time will need to be kept in a shed, cellar or larder where a low temperature can be maintained. It should be frost-proof, mice-free and well ventilated. Care should be take to ensure that no chemicals or root vegetables are stored close by, as fruit will become tainted and pick up other odors.

The apple is the most versatile of all our fruits. From apple soup to applesauce, a myriad of apple puddings and the finale of a fresh fruit dessert, there are an infinite number of ways to enjoy this delectable fruit. Apple juice is one of the most refreshing of all fruit drinks and apples can be turned into hard cider and cider brandy. The apple's versatility lies not only in its wide range of flavors, textures and colors but also in its ability to be used for both savory and sweet dishes. Apples can complement rich meats such as pork and goose, enhance vegetable salads, yet also make delicious fruit pies and tarts.

Most of the varieties on sale are primarily eating apples, but many may also be cooked and are regarded as dual purpose. Britain, however, continues to draw a firm distinction between dessert and culinary varieties. This derives from the Victorian era, when all apples were categorized into those of the finest eating quality, which were destined for the fresh fruit dessert, and cooking apples, which were large, very acidic and too sharp ever to be eaten fresh.

Dual purpose and eating varieties, on the other hand, have much less acidity and tend to retain their shape during cooking, a property that fits them for recipes such as *Tarte aux Pommes* or *Tarte Tatin*, but their taste is sweet and mild by comparison with a traditional cooker.

Modern storage has tended to erode the notion of season but, if fruit is kept at home, the dual purpose varieties are best used for cooking early in their season, when they have their maximum acidity and then after storing and mellowing they can be eaten fresh when the flesh is sweeter.

Early season varieties ripening in the summer are only available for a short time as they do not keep and indeed are best eaten ripe from the tree. Mid-season varieties, ready to be picked in early fall will keep longer and in some cases up to December. The late season apples keep well for several months and consequently are available for a much longer period. A number of late season varieties, such as Golden Delicious, Granny Smith and Red Delicious, are now grown throughout the world – in both the northern and the southern hemispheres – and as a result are on sale all year round in our markets and supermarkets.

Ashmead's Kernel
Long-esteemed English dessert variety. Quite russetted skin. Firm, white flesh, which mellows to an intense sweet-sharp, almost fruit drop flavor. Available: Very rare.

Baldwin
Deep maroon flushed, large; multi-purpose. Keeps its shape when cooked and is recommended for pies; can be eaten fresh and was used for making hard cider. Available: Dec-Apr.

Ben Davis
Dark red, large; dual purpose with sweet, firm flesh. Available: Dec-Mar/May.

Blenheim Orange
Netted with russet and orange-red flush and stripes, it was favored by Victorians for making "*Apple Charlotte*," while smaller specimens were allowed to mellow and develop a characteristic crumbly texture and nutty flavor. Fresh Blenheim Orange apples go well with cheese. When cooked, it forms a stiff purée or retains its shape. Grown under the name Bénédictin in Normandy, France where it is valued for making "*Tarte aux Pommes*"

and "*Tarte Tatin*." Available: Rare.

Braeburn
Red flushed and striped over greenish yellow with crisp to firm flesh and refreshing, fruity, quite perfumed taste. Available: Almost all year.

Bramley's Seedling

Bramley's Seedling
The best known English culinary variety is large and green, with a slight flush. Cooks to a juicy purée with plenty of strong acidity and flavor, which is ideally suited to pies, applesauce, dumplings and baked apple. Available: Rare.

Charles Ross
Handsomely flushed and striped in orange and red.

Dual purpose, cooked slices will retain their shape with a sweet, quite delicate flavor. Later in its season it makes a sweet, aromatic eater. Available: Very rare.

Cox's Orange Pippin
England's most celebrated dessert variety. Flushed and striped in orange and red with a rich, intense, complex, aromatic flavor; sweet yet with plenty of balancing acidity and a deep cream-colored, juicy flesh. Can be cooked – slices will retain shape, with a delicate flavor. Available: New Zealand imports; May-July.

Cox's Orange Pippin

Crispin syn. Mutsu
Large, greenish yellow turning gold with crisp, deep creamy

flesh. Honeyed flavor at its best, very like Golden Delicious, but larger and with a coarser texture. When cooked, slices retain shape, with a sweet, very light taste.
Available: Dec-Mar.

Delicious
Dark red with prominently crowned shape and the most widely grown of all varieties. Sweet, juicy, cream tinged green flesh, but often rather insipid; tough skin. Red Delicious, Starking, Red Chief are more highly colored forms.
Available: All year.

Discovery
Bright red flush. Crisp, juicy flesh with a hint of strawberry flavor in well-ripened fruit.
Available: Rare.

Discovery

Early Victoria
syn. Emneth Early
Pale greenish yellow. Cooking to a brisk, fruity, juicy fluff. Well suited to summer desserts such as "*Apple Snow;*" when baked will puff up like a soufflé.
Available: Very rare.

Early Victoria

Egremont Russet
"Russet" of the UK high street, with a distinctive taste – nutty, yet almost smoky and sweet, quite firm flesh.
Available: Rare.

Ellison's Orange
Flushed and striped in orange and red. Juicy, brisk, quite soft flesh with a distinct aniseed flavor in the well-ripened fruit.
Available: Rare.

Empire
Red flush and waxy bloom. Crisp, juicy, sweet with quite scented flavor.
Available: Nov-Feb.

Fiesta
Attractive, orange red flush and stripes. Sweet, crisp flesh and plenty of rich flavor recalling its Cox's Orange Pippin parent.
Available: Rare.

Fortune
syn. Laxton's Fortune
Red flushed and striped. Juicy, sweet, quite rich and lightly aromatic at its best.
Available: Rare.

Fuji
Pretty orange red flush. Crisp, firm, quite juicy flesh with honeyed sweetness.
Available: Almost all year.

Gala
Bright pink red flush and stripes over gold. Crisp, sweet flesh with a rich, honeyed, perfumed quality. Red Gala and Tenroy are more highly colored forms.
Available: Almost all year.

Golden Delicious
At best, sweet and honeyed with crisp, very juicy nearly yellow

flesh, but low in balancing acidity and can often taste flat and cloying. Dual purpose in many countries; when cooked keeps its shape well, with a light, sweet taste.
Available: All year.

Granny Smith
Bright green with brisk, crisp flesh, but often hard and acidic. Can be dual purpose; when cooked retains shape, but has mild flavor.
Available: All year.

Granny Smith

Gravenstein
Red flush over pale yellow, having a large, angular shape. Very juicy flesh and refreshing savory taste. Can be dual purpose; slices retain shape when cooked and have a sweet, delicate taste; also used for juice.
Available Sept-Oct.

Gravenstein

Grimes Golden
Sweet, juicy, crisp yellow flesh that recalls its offspring Golden Delicious, but has a better, more complex flavor. Can be cooked; slices keep their shape.
Available: Nov-Feb.

Howgate Wonder
Large, red flushed and striped. Keeps its shape when cooked with a light taste but insipid in comparison to Bramley. Later in season, eaten fresh has a juicy, sweet and pleasant flavor.
Available: Rare.

Idared
Bright red flushed with sprightly taste, but can be flavorless and chewy. Dual purpose in USA and Europe; when cooked, slices will retain shape.
Available: Nov-Jun.

James Grieve
Red flush and stripes over pale yellow. Savory, juicy, crisp yet melting flesh with strong acidity. Makes good juice and cooks well – as slices keep their shape with a sweet, delicate taste. Available: Rare.

Jerseymac
Dark red flush and bloom of its McIntosh ancestor, but ripening earlier. Perfumed, sweet vinous flavor and sweet, melting, snow white flesh; tough skin.
Available: Sept-Nov.

Jonagold
Orange red flush and red stripes over gold; often quite large. Rich, honeyed flavor, sweet and well balanced by acidity with crisp, juicy flesh. Well suited to fresh fruit and

vegetable salads. Jonagored is a more highly colored form of Jonagold.
Available: Nov-April.

Jonagold

Jonathan
Bright crimson flush; crisp, sweet with plenty of refreshing acidity. Valued also for cooking in sauces and pies; slices will retain shape.
Available: Nov-Mar.

Kidd's Orange Red
Deep pink crimson flush and stripes. Rich blend of sugar and acidity with intense aromatic flavor which mellows to a flowery rose petal quality, but in a poor year can be less interesting.
Available: Rare.

Laxton's Superb
Deep red to purple flush over greenish yellow. Sweet, juicy finely textured flesh and some aromatic quality recalling its Cox parent.
Available: Rare.

Lobo
Deep maroon flushed McIntosh type with sweet, juicy, melting flesh.
Available: Rare.

Lodi
Pale greenish yellow, cooking to a sweet, very juicy, froth.
Available: Late July-Aug.

Lodi

Lord Derby
Large, greenish yellow, angular shaped cooker. Strong, quite sharp taste when cooked and keeping a little of its form; good for pies.
Available: Rare.

Lord Lambourne
Bright red flush and stripes over greenish yellow. Crisp, juicy flesh with plenty of fruity flavor.
Available: Rare.

Macoun
Purplish red flush with heavy bloom like its McIntosh parent. Juicy, very sweet, pure white flesh perfumed from anything between a strawberry to a vinous flavor.
Available: Oct-Dec/Feb.

Malling Kent
Dark orange red flush and stripes over greenish yellow. Quite rich and aromatic, but often less interesting. Can be dual purpose; slices will retain shape when cooked with sweet, light taste.
Available: Rare.

McIntosh
Canada's most famous apple variety with a deep purplish red flush and a pronounced bloom.

Melting, juicy, white flesh
with a sweet, strawberry flavor
turning vinous later.
Available: Oct-Jan and later.

Melrose
Shiny red with brisk refreshing
taste and crisp, juicy flesh.
Melrose can be used early
in the season for cooking and
slices will retain their shape.
Available: Nov-Mar.

Melrose

Newton Wonder
Large, orange red flush over
greenish yellow. Cooks to a

sharp juicy purée, but not as
acidic as a Bramley. Suitable
for all types of baked desserts –
pies, dumplings, baked apple
and sauces. Mellows in a garden
store to become a brisk eating
apple; also good for mixed
vegetable salads.
Available: Rare.

Newtown Pippin
Greenish yellow with crisp
flesh and brisk taste which
mellows in a home store to
a distinct pineapple flavor.
Valued also for cooking,
keeping its shape, with a
sweet good taste.
Available: Dec-Mar.

Northern Spy
Large, flushed dark red with a
brisk, intense fruity flavor and
crisp flesh. Dual purpose; slices
keep shape when cooked.
Available: Nov-Mar.

Reine des Reinettes
Flushed and striped in orange
and red over gold. Multipurpose
apple – used for cooking and
favored for the famous "*Tarte
aux Pommes*," also for making
hard cider in Normandy.
Known as King of the Pippins
in the UK, Gold Parmäne in
Germany.
Available: Rare.

Rhode Island Greening
Large, greenish yellow. When
cooked, keeps shape with a sweet,
good flavor; favored for pies and
sauces. Mellows to become a
juicy, sprightly eater.
Available: Dec-Apr.

Rhode Island Greening

Ribston Pippin
The most popular Victorian
dessert apple and probable
parent of the well known Cox.
Orange flush and red stripes over
gold, patched with russet. Rich,
intensely aromatic flavor, like a
more robust Cox, with deep
cream flesh.
Available: Rare.

Rome Beauty
Deep red flush and stripes. Dual purpose. Keeps shape when cooked, sweet but mildly flavored.
Available: Dec-Apr.

Saint Edmund's Pippin
syn. St Edmund's Russet
Light golden russet. Sweet, juicy, very rich densely textured, pale cream flesh.
Available: Rare.

Saint Edmund's Pippin

Spartan
Deep maroon flush with bloom. At best, perfumed, sweet flavor like a cross between a melon and a strawberry, but often rather bland; crisp juicy white flesh. Skin rather tough but the color makes an attractive contrast in fruit salads.
Available: Nov-Mar.

Stayman's Winesap
Deep red skin like Winesap with juicy pale yellow flesh and a sprightly quality. Can be dual purpose.
Available: Jan-Mar.

Sturmer Pippin
Orange brown flush over greenish yellow. Crisp, juicy flesh, quite sweet, yet plenty of acidity and strong characteristic taste. Sturmer Pippin can be cooked and slices keep their shape.
Available: Rare.

Tydeman's Early Worcester
syn. Tydeman's Early
Bright crimson with darker stripes. Very juicy, white flesh with some strawberry flavor when really ripe.
Available: Aug-Sept.

Wealthy
Bright red flush and stripes with sweet, soft, juicy flesh.
Available: Sept-Dec.

White Transparent
or Yellow Transparent
Pale yellow in color, ripening by mid-July. Cooks to a sweet purée and also makes a refreshing, soft-fleshed eating apple with plenty of acidity.
Available: July-Aug.

Winesap
Dark red flush; sweet, juicy and fruity. Dual purpose in the US.
Available: Dec-Mar.

Worcester Pearmain
Perfectly ripe, bright red flushed. Sweet, strawberry flavor and firm, juicy white flesh, can often be chewy with little flavor.
Available: Rare.

Worcester Pearmain

CIDER APPLE SOUP

Serves 4-6

**1 pound eating apples, peeled,
cored and thinly sliced
2 cups vegetable or chicken stock
½ teaspoon ground cinnamon
¾ teaspoon ground ginger
2 tablespoons fresh white bread crumbs
finely grated rind and juice of 1 lemon
⅔ cup hard cider
⅔ cup milk**

FOR GARNISH:

**sour cream
a little ground cinnamon**

Place the apples in a saucepan with the vegetable or chicken stock, cinnamon, ginger, bread crumbs, lemon rind and juice. Bring to a boil, then simmer gently for 10 minutes or until the apples are soft. Reserve some slices for garnish.

Purée the soup in a blender or a food processor, or rub through a strainer. Stir in the hard cider and milk. Chill until needed. Serve in individual dishes, garnished with the reserved apple slices, sour cream and a little ground cinnamon.

MICROWAVE METHOD: Place the apples with the hot stock, cinnamon, ginger, bread crumbs and lemon in a large casserole dish. Cover and cook on High for 7-8 minutes, or until apples are soft. Finish as above.

CHESTNUT & APPLE SOUP

Serves 4

**1 pound chestnuts, skins slashed
1 tablespoon corn oil
1 onion, finely chopped
3 cups chicken stock
1¼ cups hard cider (*preferably dry*)
½ pound cooking apples, peeled,
cored and sliced
salt and freshly ground black pepper
flat-leaf parsley, for garnish**

Put the chestnuts in a large saucepan and cover with cold water. Bring to a boil and cook for 10 minutes. Drain and peel the chestnuts. Place in a clean pan, cover with water and cook for 20 minutes.

Put the oil in another large pan, add the onion and cook until soft, then add the stock, cider and apples.

Stir to mix the ingredients. Add the chestnuts with any of their cooking liquid left in the pan. Bring to a boil, reduce the heat, cover and simmer for about 15 minutes, until chestnuts are completely cooked. Work in a blender or food processor until smooth, or rub through a strainer. Season to taste and serve hot, garnished with flat-leaf parsley.

Illustrated opposite

CURRIED APPLE SOUP

Serves 4

**1 pound tart eating apples, peeled,
cored and chopped
1 onion, sliced
2 celery stalks, thinly sliced
3 tablespoons butter or margarine
2 teaspoons curry powder (*mild or hot, to taste*)
1 tablespoon chopped fresh mint
¼ cup lemon juice
2½ cups chicken stock
1¼ cups milk or plain yogurt
salt and freshly ground black pepper
4 teaspoons sunflower seeds, for garnish**

In a large saucepan, gently cook apples, onion and celery in the butter, stirring occasionally, for 5 minutes. Increase the heat to moderate, stir in the curry powder, cook for 3 minutes. Add the mint and lemon juice and stir in the stock. Bring slowly to a boil, cover and simmer for 15 minutes, or until the apples are tender.

Purée the soup in a blender or food processor, or rub through a strainer. Return soup to the rinsed pan and gradually pour in the milk or yogurt and bring slowly to simmering point. Do not let boil. Season to taste.

Serve the soup hot or cold, garnished with the sunflower seeds.

APPLE & CORIANDER SOUP

Serves 6

**¼ stick butter
1 onion, sliced
1 garlic clove, chopped
2 teaspoons ground coriander
1 potato, peeled and coarsely chopped
1½ pounds tart eating apples, peeled,
cored and chopped
4 cups chicken stock
1¼ cups cultured buttermilk
1 tablespoon lemon juice
2 tablespoons chopped fresh cilantro or mint
¼ cup pot cheese or cottage cheese
salt and freshly ground black pepper
fresh cilantro or mint sprigs, for garnish**

Melt the butter in a saucepan, cook the onion and garlic over a moderate heat for 2 minutes. Stir in the coriander and cook for 1 minute longer, stirring. Add the potato and apples, stir well and cook for 2-3 minutes. Pour on the stock, stirring all the time, and then the buttermilk. Season to taste.

Bring to a boil, cover; simmer for 15 minutes. Stir in the lemon juice and cilantro or mint. Purée the soup in a blender or food processor, or rub through a strainer. Reheat the soup gently, adjust the seasoning if necessary. Serve topped with spoonfuls of pot cheese, garnished with sprigs of cilantro or mint.

TURKEY KABOBS WITH APPLE

Serves 6

KABOBS:

**6 turkey cutlets,
total weight about 1½ pounds
6 bacon slices halved lengthwise
2 small green eating apples, each cut
into 6 wedges
1 sweet red, orange or yellow pepper, cored,
seeded and cut into 1-inch squares
1 sweet green pepper, cored, seeded and cut
into 1-inch squares
12 large cherry tomatoes, or 6 tomatoes, halved
thyme sprigs, for garnish**

MARINADE:

**2 teaspoons paprika
⅓ cup olive oil
2 teaspoons dried thyme
salt and freshly ground black pepper**

Cut each turkey cutlet crosswise into four wide strips and place in a large shallow dish. To make the marinade, mix together the paprika, olive oil, dried thyme, and salt and pepper. Add to the turkey, making sure to thoroughly coat the turkey pieces. Cover the dish and leave to marinate in the refrigerator for 1 hour.

After marinating, fold the strips of turkey two or three times to form squares, each about 1-inch. Wrap a piece of bacon around half of these turkey squares.

Oil six long skewers and thread an apple wedge on to each. Continue to assemble the kabobs alternating between the squares of bacon-wrapped turkey, plain turkey, peppers and the tomatoes, ending each kabob with an apple wedge.

Cook the kabobs over a hot barbecue, or under a preheated hot broiler for 12-15 minutes, or until the turkey juices run clear, turning them over several times during cooking and brushing them with the remaining marinade.

Serve the kabobs with a rice salad, and garnish with sprigs of thyme.

ROAST PHEASANT FLAMBÉED WITH CALVADOS

Serves 4

**2 pheasants, preferably hen birds,
plucked and cleaned ready for the oven or
2 Rock Cornish game hens
1 large onion, quartered
½ stick butter
4 tart eating apples, peeled,
cored and thickly sliced
¼ cup all-purpose flour
1¼ cups dry white wine
¼ cup Calvados
⅓ cup heavy cream
2 tablespoons chopped fresh parsley
salt and freshly ground black pepper**

Place the prepared birds in a roasting pan. Tuck the onion quarters under the birds and sprinkle with a little salt and pepper. Dot with the butter and place in a preheated oven, 375°F. Roast for about 45 minutes, or until the birds are cooked through and tender.

Add the apples to the pan 15-20 minutes before the end of the cooking time.

Have a warmed serving dish ready. Remove the birds from the roasting pan and transfer them to the dish. Place the apple slices in a separate dish and keep them hot while making the Calvados sauce.

Stir the flour into the pan juices and cook over a moderate heat for 1 minute. Stir in the dry white wine and bring to a boil, stirring all the time. Remove from the heat.

Heat the Calvados in a small saucepan until it is just warm, ignite it and then, when the flames die down, add it to the sauce. Stir in the heavy cream and chopped parsley and adjust the seasoning to taste, then reheat the sauce gently without boiling.

Pour a little of the sauce around the pheasants and arrange the apples in the dish. Serve the birds accompanied by potato chips and fresh green vegetables, with the remaining sauce served separately.

Illustrated opposite

BAKED CHICKEN WITH APPLES

Serves 4

⅓ cup raisins
½ stick butter
4 chicken pieces
1 pound eating apples, such as
Granny Smiths, peeled, cored and sliced
2 tablespoons lemon juice
⅓ cup dry vermouth
1 teaspoon ground cinnamon
½ cup heavy cream
salt and freshly ground black pepper

Soak the raisins for 1 hour in warm water. Heat half the butter in a skillet and brown the chicken pieces on all sides. Remove to a plate and season well.

Add the remaining butter and apple slices to the skillet and brown lightly. Place half the apples in the bottom of a casserole dish and arrange the chicken on top.

Mix the lemon juice, vermouth, salt and pepper, cinnamon and drained raisins. Place the remaining apples around the chicken, season and pour the raisin mixture over the chicken and apples. Cover and bake in a preheated oven, 325°F, for about 1 hour. Stir in the cream and return to the oven to heat through for 5 minutes. Adjust the seasoning to taste and serve.

TROUT WITH APPLES

Serves 4

4 large rainbow trout, cleaned
1 tablespoon lemon juice
4 rosemary sprigs
¾ stick butter
2 eating apples, cored and thickly sliced
freshly ground black pepper

FOR GARNISH:

1 lemon, quartered
chopped fresh parsley

Sprinkle the inside of each trout with plenty of pepper and the lemon juice and place a sprig of rosemary in the cavity.

Melt ½ stick of the butter in a large skillet, add the trout and cook over a moderate heat for about 12-15 minutes until tender. Using a wooden spatula, turn the fish over once during cooking, taking care not to break the skin. Transfer to a warm serving dish. Add the remaining butter to the pan and cook the apples. Cook for a further 4-5 minutes, turning the apples once, until golden.

Serve the fish surrounded by the apples and garnished with the lemon wedges that have been dipped in parsley.

PORK CHOPS NORMANDY-STYLE

Serves 4

4 loin pork chops, 1-inch thick, trimmed of fat
1 tablespoon corn oil
¼ stick butter
2 onions, sliced
1 garlic clove, crushed
2 small cooking apples, peeled, cored and sliced
1 tablespoon all-purpose flour
1 cup apple cider
1 tablespoon honey
1 tablespoon brandy (*optional*)
1 teaspoon fresh chopped thyme
¼ cup heavy cream
salt and freshly ground black pepper

Cook chops in the oil in a skillet over a moderately high heat for 3 minutes each side. Transfer to a casserole dish. Add half the butter to the skillet, cook onions and garlic over a moderate heat for 3 minutes. Transfer to casserole dish. Cook apple slices in a skillet for 1 minute each side and add to casserole.

Melt remaining butter, stir in the flour, cook for a few seconds in the skillet. Stir in the cider, honey and brandy, if using. Bring to a boil, stirring constantly. Season to taste. Add to the casserole with the thyme. Cover and cook in a preheated oven, 375°F, for 35 minutes. Skim off the surface fat, stir in the cream. Adjust seasoning to taste and serve.

PORK & APPLE PASTIES

Serves 4

½ pound ground lean pork, finely cubed
1 small cooking apple, peeled, cored and grated
1 onion, chopped
½ teaspoon dried sage
2 tablespoons hard cider or chicken stock
salt and freshly ground black pepper
milk, to glaze
DOUGH:
2 cups all-purpose plain flour
pinch of salt
1 stick margarine
2-3 tablespoons cold water

For the dough place flour and salt in a bowl. Cut up the margarine and rub in until the mixture resembles fine bread crumbs. Sprinkle 2 tablespoons of water over and mix to form a dough, adding extra water, if necessary. Knead lightly and chill.

Mix together the remaining ingredients and season to taste. Divide dough into four and roll each piece out to a 6-inch circle. Divide filling among circles, dampen edges with water and bring together over the filling. Seal, pleat edges and place on greased baking sheet. Brush with milk, bake in preheated oven, 400°F, for 20 minutes. Reduce heat to 350°F, bake for further 20-30 minutes. Serve hot.

APPLE, DATE & CELERY SALAD

Serves 4

1 bunch celery stalks, sliced into ½-inch pieces
⅔ cup thinly sliced dates
½ pound tart eating apples, cored and cut
into ½-inch cubes
¼ cup chopped pistachio nuts

DRESSING:

2 tablespoons honey
1¼ cups plain yogurt
1 tablespoon finely chopped fresh mint

Place the sliced celery, dates and apple cubes in a salad bowl.

For the dressing, combine the honey, yogurt and mint in a small bowl. Pour over the celery and fruit and toss gently.

Serve the salad chilled, sprinkled with chopped pistachio nuts.

ORCHARD SALAD

Serves 4-6

grated rind and juice of 2 small oranges
1 tablespoon chopped fresh mint or parsley
3 firm pears, quartered, cored and sliced
2 eating apples, quartered, cored and sliced
1 cup blackberries or blueberries
½ cup red currants
½ cup coarsely chopped roasted hazelnuts
salt and freshly ground black pepper
salad leaves, to serve

Place the orange rind and orange juice in a mixing bowl. Stir in the mint or parsley and season to taste. Add the sliced pears and apples and toss well.

Add the blackberries or blueberries, red currants and hazelnuts, toss all together and serve on a bed of salad leaves.

Serve the salad as an accompaniment to rich meats such as pork or duck.

Illustrated opposite

HERRING & APPLE SALAD

Serves 4

1 pound kippered herring fillets
3 tablespoons lemon juice
2 teaspoons corn oil
1 teaspoon ground coriander (*optional*)
⅓ cup long-grain brown rice, washed
2 cups water
2 tablespoons chopped fresh parsley
1 large red eating apple, cored and diced
pinch of freshly ground black pepper

TO SERVE:

1 head of leaf-lettuce, about 1 pound
1 lemon, cut into wedges

Poach the kippered herring fillets for 5 minutes in simmering water to cover. Drain, scrape off the skin and cut into bite-size pieces. Place in a serving dish and pour over the lemon juice, oil and coriander, if using. Chill for 3-4 hours, stirring occasionally.

Bring the rice and water to a boil in a saucepan. Cover and simmer 35-45 minutes, until the rice is tender. Drain well. Rinse in hot water and drain again. Combine the rice while still warm with the parsley and pepper.

To serve, shred the lettuce leaves and divide among four plates. Top with spoonfuls of rice and arrange pieces of apple and kippered herring on top. Garnish with lemon wedges.

CHICKEN & APPLE CURRY MAYONNAISE

Serves 4-6

1 pound boneless, skinless cooked chicken
or turkey, cut into cubes (*about 2 cups*)
2 red eating apples, cut into small cubes
3 tablespoons golden raisins
3 tablespoons roasted, salted peanuts
6 tablespoons mayonnaise
1 teaspoon medium or mild curry powder
½ teaspoon mild chili powder
1 tablespoon lime or lemon juice
salt and freshly ground black pepper
crisp lettuce leaves, to serve
cilantro leaves, for garnish

Place all the ingredients, except the salt, pepper, lettuce leaves and cilantro in a large mixing bowl and mix thoroughly. Season to taste with salt and pepper.

Line a serving dish or individual serving dishes with the lettuce leaves and spoon in the curried chicken mixture. Garnish with the cilantro leaves.

APPLE & AVOCADO PASTA SALAD

Serves 4-6

**2 cups small pasta shapes, such as
bows, shells or twists
1 teaspoon corn oil
1 avocado
2 tablespoons lemon juice
3 celery stalks, sliced
2 red eating apples, cored and thinly sliced
¼ cup French dressing
2 tablespoons snipped fresh chives**

Cook the pasta shapes in lightly salted boiling water with the oil, according to the package directions, until *al dente*. Drain and cool under cold water. Drain again thoroughly.

Peel and pit the avocado, then slice thinly or chop into cubes. Toss in the lemon juice to prevent it from turning brown.

Mix the cooked pasta with the avocado, celery and apples in a serving bowl. Add the dressing and chives and toss gently to coat and mix. Garnish with any extra chives.

WALDORF SALAD

Serves 6

**6 tart eating apples, peeled,
cored and cut into small cubes
3 tablespoons lemon juice, strained
1 can (*about 8 ounces*) pineapple slices in
natural juice, drained
¾ cup chopped walnuts
6 celery stalks, sliced
½ cup mayonnaise
⅓ cup sour cream
2 teaspoons honey
salt**

Place the apple cubes in a large bowl and toss with the lemon juice. Cut the pineapple into small pieces and add to the bowl with the walnuts and celery.

Combine the mayonnaise, sour cream and honey with salt to taste and fold through the apple mixture. Cover and chill for 1-2 hours to blend and mellow the flavors. Bring to room temperature to serve.

APPLE & CELERIAC SALAD

Serves 6

1 celeriac, about 1½ pounds,
peeled and quartered
2 tablespoons lemon juice
1 teaspoon salt
⅓ cup mayonnaise
1 tablespoon finely chopped fresh chervil
or borage
1 tablespoon finely chopped fresh parsley
2 crisp red eating apples, cored
and thinly sliced into rings
1 cup salted cashews, finely chopped

Put the celeriac in a saucepan, add the lemon juice and salt and cover with water. Bring to a boil, reduce the heat and cook for about 30 minutes, until tender, but still firm. Drain thoroughly, let cool, then slice thinly.

Mix together the mayonnaise, chervil or borage and parsley. Add the apple and celeriac slices and stir to coat. Transfer to a salad bowl. Sprinkle the cashews over the top and serve.

MICROWAVE METHOD: Peel the celeriac and cut into eight wedges. Place in a casserole dish. Add the lemon juice and 6 tablespoons of water. Cover and cook on High for 7-8 minutes until just tender. Drain and finish as above.

APPLE TREE SALAD

Serves 4-6

2 red eating apples, cored and thinly sliced
2 teaspoons lemon juice
2 cups thinly sliced mushrooms
½ pound red grapes, halved and seeded
2 carrots, scraped and grated
2 celery stalks, sliced
2 tablespoons roasted sesame seeds
DRESSING:
2 tablespoons olive oil
1 tablespoon apple juice
2 tablespoons sour cream
salt and freshly ground black pepper

Mix all the dressing ingredients together until well blended.

Toss the apples in the lemon juice. Mix together the apple and mushroom slices, the grapes, carrots and celery. Sprinkle with the sesame seeds.

Pour on the dressing and mix well to serve. Alternatively, serve the dressing separately.

Illustrated opposite

APPLE & SWEET POTATO CASSEROLE

Serves 4-6

2 sweet potatoes, about 2 pounds
4 small apples, cored and sliced into rings
2-3 tablespoons sugar
2 tablespoons coarsely chopped pecans
or cashews
½ stick butter
1 teaspoon salt
pinch of ground nutmeg

Place the whole sweet potatoes in a large saucepan, cover with boiling water, bring back to a boil, lower the heat and cook for about 25-30 minutes or until barely tender. Rinse under cold water, peel and cut lengthwise into thick slices.

Fill a greased ovenproof dish with alternate layers of sweet potato and apple and sprinkle with the sugar and nuts.

Melt the butter in a small pan, season with the salt and the nutmeg and pour over the sweet potato and apple mixture.

Cook in a preheated oven, 400°F, for about 20-25 minutes. Serve immediately as a tasty vegetable dish, perfect with crisp roast pork.

APPLE & RED CABBAGE

Serves 8

1 head red cabbage, about 3 pounds,
finely shredded
¼ cup diced fat salted pork, or ½ stick butter
2 Spanish onions, thinly sliced
2 tablespoons brown sugar
2 tart eating apples, peeled,
cored and chopped
⅓ cup vegetable stock
⅔ cup red wine
3 tablespoons red wine vinegar
1 small raw beet, coarsely grated
salt and freshly ground black pepper

Cover the cabbage with boiling water and set aside. In a large heavy-bottom saucepan, sauté pork until the fat runs, or melt the butter. Add onions, cook, stirring frequently, until soft and transparent. Stir in the sugar and continue to cook gently until the onions are caramelized and golden. Take care not to let the sugar burn.

Drain cabbage well. Add it to the pan with apples, stock, wine and vinegar. Mix well and season generously. Cover tightly and cook gently for 1½ hours, stirring occasionally. Mix in the grated beet – this transforms the color – and continue to cook, covered, for 30 minutes longer, or until cabbage is soft. Adjust the seasoning if necessary, and serve very hot.

APPLE & STILTON STUFFED ONIONS

Serves 4

4 large onions, about ½ pound each
1 large cooking apple, peeled,
cored and finely chopped
1 cup fresh bread crumbs
⅔ cup finely crumbled blue Stilton
1 bunch watercress
½ stick butter
salt and freshly ground black pepper

Peel the onions, then cook in a saucepan of boiling water for 15 minutes, until just tender. Drain and let cool so they can be handled.

Mix the apples with bread crumbs and cheese. Reserve four sprigs of watercress, trim and chop remainder and add to cheese mixture.

Remove the center of each onion – this is easiest if you gradually scoop out the layers of onion with a teaspoon. Leave an unbroken shell about two layers thick. Chop the scooped-out onion and add to the cheese mixture. Mix well and season to taste, then press the mixture into the onion shells.

Stand onions in an ovenproof dish, dot with a little butter. Bake in a preheated oven, 350°F, for 45 minutes, or until stuffing is cooked through. Serve garnished with reserved watercress sprigs.

FENNEL BRAISED WITH APPLE

Serves 4

2 large fennel bulbs, quartered lengthwise
1 large cooking apple, peeled, cored and sliced
⅔ cup chicken stock
1 tablespoon lemon juice
salt and freshly ground black pepper
1 tablespoon chopped parsley, for garnish

Place the fennel quarters in a casserole dish or ovenproof dish. Add the apple to the casserole dish with the chicken stock, lemon juice and salt and pepper.

Cover and bake in a preheated oven, 350°F, for 30 minutes, or until the fennel is tender, but not soft.

Drain the stock into a small saucepan and boil for about 3 minutes, or until it is reduced to 3 tablespoons. Pour the sauce over the fennel, sprinkle with chopped parsley and serve. Ideal with pork or fish.

MICROWAVE METHOD: Place the fennel, stock and lemon juice in a casserole dish. Cover and cook on High for 7 minutes. Add the apple, re-cover and cook on High for 3-4 minutes or until fennel is just tender. Season. Pour over 3-4 tablespoons of juices and serve, sprinkled with parsley.

FRENCH APPLE PIE

Serves 4-6

DOUGH:

1¼ cups all-purpose flour
pinch of salt
⅓ cup butter, cut into small pieces
1 tablespoon sugar
2 teaspoons ground almonds
1 egg yolk
2-3 tablespoons cold water

FILLING:

1 pound cooking apples, cooked without
sugar and puréed
¼ cup sugar
grated rind of ½ lemon
2 cooking apples, peeled, cored and thinly sliced

GLAZE:

1 tablespoon lemon juice
2-3 tablespoons confectioners' sugar

To make the dough sift the flour and salt into a bowl, cut in the butter and using your fingertips, rub the fat and flour together until it resembles fine bread crumbs; add the sugar and almonds. Stir in the egg yolk and enough cold water to mix to a stiff dough. Tip out onto a floured surface and knead lightly for 1 minute. Wrap in plastic wrap and chill in the refrigerator for 30 minutes.

Roll out the dough on a floured surface and use to line an 8-inch tart pan, set on a baking sheet or an 8-inch springform pie pan.

Add the sugar and lemon rind to the apple purée and spoon into the pie shell. Arrange the sliced apples neatly over the surface. Brush them with lemon juice and sprinkle with the confectioners' sugar.

Bake the pie in a preheated oven, 425°F, for about 25-30 minutes or until the pastry and the apples are golden brown.

Serve warm or cold with whipped cream.

Illustrated opposite

FARMHOUSE FRUIT PIE

Serves 6

PIE DOUGH:

1½ cups all-purpose flour
pinch of salt
¾ stick butter or margarine, cut
into small pieces
1½-2 tablespoons water

FILLING:

2 cooking apples, peeled, cored and thinly sliced
2 pears, peeled, cored and thinly sliced
2 tablespoons light corn syrup
1 tablespoon red currant jelly, melted
¼ teaspoon apple pie spice
⅓ cup golden raisins
2 tablespoons soft brown sugar

TOPPING:

about ½ pound frozen puff pastry, thawed
beaten egg, to glaze

To make the pie dough, sift the flour and salt into a large bowl, cut in the butter or margarine and rub in until the mixture resembles fine bread crumbs. Add enough water to form a firm dough. Knead lightly until it is smooth and free from cracks.

Roll out dough on a lightly floured surface to a round large enough to line the base and sides of an 8-inch fluted springform pie pan, allowing the dough to over-hang the edge of the pan slightly. Chill until needed.

To make the filling, mix the sliced apples and pears with the corn syrup, red currant jelly, spice, golden raisins and brown sugar. Spoon into the pie shell.

For the topping, roll out the puff pastry to a round large enough to cover the pie. Dampen the edge of the dough in the pan and place the puff pastry lid in position. Seal the edges together well then trim neatly. Flute the edges.

Glaze the pastry with beaten egg then lightly cut into it to give a lattice pattern, using a sharp pointed knife. Reroll the puff pastry trimmings and cut into leaf shapes for decoration. Position the leaves on the pie and brush with beaten egg.

Cook on a preheated baking sheet in a preheated oven, 400°F, for 35-40 minutes until the pastry is risen and golden brown. Cover with foil, reduce the heat to 350°F, and continue cooking for a further 15 minutes.

Cool slightly in the pan on a wire tray, then remove the sides of the pan, leaving the pie on the base. Serve hot or cold with custard, cream or ice cream.

APPLE MERINGUE PIE

Serves 4-6

**1 pound cooking apples, peeled,
cored and sliced**
⅔ cup sugar
¼ stick butter
grated rind of 1 lemon
⅔ cup water
2 eggs, separated

DOUGH:

1½ cups all-purpose flour
pinch of salt
¾ stick butter or margarine
1½-2 tablespoons water

To make the dough, sift the flour and salt into a bowl. Cut in the fat, and rub it in until the mixture resembles fine bread crumbs. Add enough water to form a firm dough. Knead lightly until smooth and free from cracks.

Roll out the dough on a lightly floured work surface to a round large enough to line the base and sides of an 8-inch fluted springform pie pan.

Bake as follows. Line the pie shell with waxed paper and cover with a layer of dry beans to prevent the base blistering. Place in a preheated oven, 400°F, for 10-15 minutes until the sides of the pie shell are set and golden. Remove the lining paper and beans (which can be reused) and return the pie shell to the oven for about 5 minutes or until the base is crisp. Let the pie shell cool.

Put the apples in a saucepan with ¼ cup of the sugar, the butter, lemon rind and water. Cook gently until the apples are tender, then beat to a smooth purée.

Cool the mixture slightly, then beat in the egg yolks. Put the mixture into the pie shell. Place in the oven and bake at 350°F, for 20 minutes.

Whisk the egg whites until stiff, whisk in the remaining sugar, then spread the meringue over the top of the apples. Return to the oven for 15-20 minutes until golden. Serve hot or cold with light cream.

APPLE & BERRY CRUMB PIE

Serves 6-8

DOUGH:

1½ cups all-purpose flour

pinch of salt

¾ stick butter or margarine,
cut into small pieces

1½-2 tablespoons water

FILLING:

3 cups thickly sliced peeled apples

1½ cups cranberries

½ cup sugar

1½ cups all-purpose flour

¾ stick butter

¾ teaspoon ground cinnamon

½ teaspoon grated lemon rind

½ cup firmly packed brown sugar

LIQUEUR CREAM:

1⅔ cups heavy cream

sifted confectioners' sugar, to taste

Cointreau, Grand Marnier or
other liqueur, to taste

To make the dough sift the flour and salt into a bowl, cut in the fat and rub in until the mixture resembles fine bread crumbs. Add enough water to form a firm dough. Knead lightly until smooth and free from cracks.

Roll out the dough on a lightly floured surface to a round large enough to line the base and sides of an 8-9-inch fluted springform pie pan. Chill until required.

For the filling, toss the apples and cranberries with the sugar and put into the pie shell. Place the flour, butter, cinnamon and lemon rind in a bowl, then rub together until crumbly. Stir in the brown sugar. Sprinkle evenly over the fruit and pat down lightly.

Bake in a preheated oven, 350°F, for about 45 minutes or until the crumb topping and pastry are golden brown.

To make the liqueur cream, whip the cream until it begins to thicken. Sweeten to taste with sifted confectioners' sugar and add a spoonful or two of Cointreau or other liqueur to taste, then continue whipping until thick. Serve pie warm or cold, with liqueur cream.

Illustrated opposite

APPLE & APRICOT BRAID

Serves 6-8

about ½ pound frozen puff pastry, thawed
5 fresh apricots, halved,
pitted and quartered
1 large cooking apple, peeled, cored and diced
2 tablespoons sugar
½ cup slivered almonds
1 egg, beaten
1 tablespoon soft brown sugar
sifted confectioners' sugar, to serve

Roll out pastry to a rectangle 9 x 12 inches in size. Make diagonal slashes at ¾-inch intervals along both sides of the length of the rectangle, leaving a 4-inch panel down the center.

Mix together the fruit, sugar and almonds, and spread down center panel. Turn two ends of the pastry in, then braid pastry strips over filling, securing the last two strips under the braid with beaten egg.

Place on a baking sheet, brush with beaten egg and sprinkle with brown sugar. Bake in a preheated oven, 400°F, for 20 minutes, until well risen, then reduce the heat to 350°F, and continue cooking for 15-20 minutes, until golden. Dust with confectioners' sugar and serve with whipped cream.

SPICED APPLE TURNOVERS

Serves 6

4 large cooking apples, peeled,
cored and chopped
⅔ cup firmly packed soft brown sugar
1 teaspoon ground cinnamon
1 tablespoon raisins
about ½ pound frozen puff pastry, thawed
beaten egg yolk, to glaze

Cook the apples, sugar, cinnamon and raisins in a little water until the mixture forms a compôte. Allow to cool.

Roll out the puff pastry and cut out six 6-inch circles. Brush the edges with water. Spoon the cold apple into the center of each circle. Fold and seal the edges of the pastry, enclosing the apple, and crimp the edges neatly. Brush the top of each turnover with lightly beaten egg yolk and decorate with the point of a sharp knife.

Put the turnovers on a baking sheet sprinkled with water, and bake in a preheated oven, 425°F, for 20 minutes. Serve hot or cold with whipped cream.

CREAM & APPLE PIE

Serves 6-8

DOUGH:

2 cups all-purpose flour

pinch of salt

1 stick butter or margarine

2-3 tablespoons water

CUSTARD CREAM:

3 tablespoons sugar

pinch of salt

3 tablespoons cornstarch

⅔ cup milk

⅔ cup light cream

3 egg yolks, lightly beaten

1 tablespoon brandy, apricot or orange liqueur, or 1 teaspoon vanilla extract

⅔ cup heavy cream

APPLES:

1 tablespoon brandy

1 teaspoon lemon juice

2 tablespoons cold water

4 large, fragrant eating apples, peeled, cored and very thinly sliced

2 tablespoons melted butter

2 tablespoons sugar, sifted

Make the pie shell and bake without filling as described on page 31, using a fluted 10-inch springform pie pan.

For the custard cream, mix the sugar, salt and the cornstarch together in a heavy-bottom saucepan and stir in the milk and light cream. Bring the mixture to a boil, stirring, then simmer for 3-4 minutes. Remove the pan from the heat and cool the mixture slightly, stirring. Then gradually beat in the egg yolks.

Return the pan to a very low heat and cook, stirring constantly, for 3-4 minutes or until the custard is very thick and smooth. Do not let the custard bubble. Stir in the brandy, liqueur or vanilla. Cool, beating occasionally to prevent a skin from forming on top. Set aside in a covered bowl until ready to use.

For the apples, mix the brandy, lemon juice and water in a large bowl. Coat the apples in the brandy mixture.

Whip the heavy cream stiffly and fold it into the custard. Spread the custard cream over the base of the cooked pie shell. Arrange the apple slices in overlapping concentric circles over the top, shaking them free of excess moisture as you lift them out of the bowl. Brush the apples with melted butter; dust with sugar.

Place pie under a moderate broiler and broil steadily for 10 minutes, or until the surface is golden and lightly caramelized. Regulate the heat of the broiler so that the sides of the pie shell do not get too brown before the top is caramelized, or shield the dough with a little crumpled foil. Serve lukewarm, cold or chilled, on the day it is made.

APPLE STRUDEL

Serves 8-10

DOUGH:

2 cups all-purpose flour
½ teaspoon salt
1 egg, lightly beaten
2 tablespoons corn oil
3 tablespoons warm water

FILLING:

1 stick butter
1 cup fresh white bread crumbs
1½ pounds cooking apples, peeled,
cored and coarsely grated
⅓ cup raisins
⅓ cup dried currants
⅓ cup sugar
½ teaspoon ground cinnamon
2 teaspoons finely grated lemon rind
sifted confectioners' sugar, to serve

Sift the flour and salt together. Make a well in the center and pour in the egg and oil. Add the water gradually, stirring with a fork, to make a soft sticky dough. Work the dough in the bowl until it leaves the sides clean, then tip out onto a lightly floured surface and knead for about 15 minutes or until the dough feels smooth and elastic. Form into a ball, place in a bowl and cover with a warm cloth. Leave to rest for 1 hour.

Melt half the butter in a saucepan and cook the bread crumbs until they are crisp and golden. Add the apples, raisins, dried currants, superfine sugar, cinnamon and lemon rind.

Warm a rolling pin, and flour a large clean dish towel. Place the dough on the towel and roll it out to a rectangle as thinly as possible, lifting and turning it to prevent it from sticking to the cloth. Using the backs of your hands, gently stretch the dough, working from the center to the outside until it is paper thin – you should be able to read through the dough, but to do this takes years of practice and patience. Then leave the dough to rest for 15 minutes.

Melt the remaining butter and use most of it to brush all over the dough. Spread the filling on the dough to within 1 inch of the edges. Lift the two corners of the dish towel nearest to you and roll the dough away from you. Place the dough on a greased baking sheet and form into a horseshoe. Brush all over with the remaining melted butter. Bake in a preheated oven, 400°F, for about 20 minutes, then reduce the heat to 350°F, for a further 30 minutes.

Serve warm or cold, dusted with confectioners' sugar and cut into thick slices.

Illustrated opposite

BAKED APPLES
WITH DATES

Serves 4

4 large cooking apples, cored
⅓ cup chopped dates
3 tablespoons raisins
8 almonds, chopped
2 tablespoons soft brown sugar
½ teaspoon ground cinnamon
¼ cup apple cider

Make a shallow cut around the middle of each cooking apple.

Mix together the dates, raisins, almonds, sugar and cinnamon and use to fill the apple cavities, pressing down firmly.

Place in an ovenproof dish and add the cider. Bake in a preheated oven, 350°F, for about 50-60 minutes, until soft. Serve hot with cream or custard.

MICROWAVE METHOD: Prepare apples as above and place in a shallow dish. Add the cider. Cover loosely with waxed paper and cook on High for 7-9 minutes or until fruit is just cooked but still holds shape. Rearrange the apples after 4 minutes. Leave to stand for about 5 minutes before serving.

Illustrated on page 1

APPLE & LEMON
SPONGE PUDDING

Serves 6

2 cups thinly sliced, peeled cooking apples
⅔ cup sugar
6 tablespoons tub margarine
½ cup self-rising flour
2 eggs, separated
grated rind and juice of 1 large lemon
¾-1 cup milk

Place the apples in a 6-cup ovenproof dish. Sprinkle with 2 tablespoons of the sugar.

Beat the remaining sugar with the margarine. Stir in the flour, egg yolks, lemon rind and juice and mix well. Gradually mix in the milk. Whisk the egg whites until stiff but not dry. Fold into the lemon mixture and then pour over the apples.

Bake in a preheated oven, 325°F, for about 45 minutes, until golden brown – the pudding separates to give a fluffy sponge topping over an apple base. Serve warm with light cream.

CREPES AUX POMMES

Makes 8

¾ stick butter
4 small eating apples, peeled,
cored and sliced
2 tablespoons confectioners' sugar

BATTER:

2⅔ cups all-purpose flour
2 eggs, lightly beaten
⅔ cup milk
1½ tablespoons melted butter

To make the batter, sift the flour into a bowl. Beat in eggs one at a time. Beat in milk until you obtain a smooth batter, then whisk in the butter. Let stand for 2 hours before using.

For each apple pancake, melt a pat of butter in an 8-inch skillet. Arrange one eighth of the sliced apples in the pan. Cook on one side until soft and golden, then turn the slices over and cook the other side.

Pour enough pancake batter into the pan to cover the bottom. Cook one side and turn carefully. While the second side is cooking, sprinkle a little confectioners' sugar over the pancake. Slide it onto a dessert plate and glaze under a hot broiler for a few seconds. Repeat with the rest of the apples and batter. Serve warm with cream or ice cream.

APPLE NUT CRISP

Serves 4

4 large dessert apples, about 1¾ pounds
peeled, cored and coarsely chopped
5 tablespoons light brown sugar
¾ cup whole wheat flour
¾ cup all-purpose flour
½ teaspoon ground cardamom (*optional*)
½ teaspoon apple pie spice
1 teaspoon ground cinnamon
¼ teaspoon ground nutmeg
⅓ cup softened butter
½ cup chopped shelled Brazil nuts

Place the apples in a large bowl, sprinkle with 1 tablespoon of the sugar and set aside.

Mix the flours and spices together in a large mixing bowl. Cut and rub in the butter until the mixture resembles fine bread crumbs. Stir in the remaining sugar.

Line the bottom of a buttered ovenproof dish with one-third of the flour mixture. Put the apples and any juice on top. Sprinkle with the remaining flour mixture. Sprinkle over the chopped Brazil nuts.

Cover with foil and bake in a preheated oven, 400°F, for 35 minutes, removing the foil for the last 10 minutes. Serve hot with custard.

TARTE TATIN

Serves 6

DOUGH:

1½ cups all-purpose flour, sifted

¾ stick butter

2 tablespoons sugar

1 egg yolk

FILLING:

½ stick butter

¼ cup sugar

2 pounds eating apples, peeled,
cored and quartered

1 teaspoon ground nutmeg, for sprinkling

To make the dough, place the flour in a bowl, cut and rub in butter until mixture resembles fine bread crumbs. Stir in sugar, then egg yolk to make a short, sweet dough. Chill briefly.

For the filling, melt butter in an 8-inch *Tarte Tatin* pan or a deep layer cake pan. Stir the sugar into the butter, cook gently until it dissolves and begins to caramelize. Remove from heat, then pack apples tightly into pan.

Roll dough into a circle slightly larger than the pan. Lift over the apples, tucking edges down into the pan. Bake in a preheated oven, 400°F, for 30 minutes, or until pastry is cooked. Invert onto a plate, sprinkle with nutmeg and serve hot or warm.

Illustrated on front jacket

CRUNCHY CINNAMON PUDDING

Serves 4

4 cups fresh bread crumbs

2-3 teaspoons ground cinnamon

½ cup firmly packed brown sugar

¾ stick butter, melted

4 cooking apples, peeled, cored and quartered

½ cup water

3 tablespoons sugar

1 cup heavy cream

⅔ cup plain yogurt

TO SERVE:

whipped cream

chocolate curls

Stir bread crumbs, cinnamon and brown sugar into the butter in a skillet and stir over a medium heat until crisp and toffee-like. Cool.

Poach apples in the water with 1 tablespoon of the sugar. When soft, purée in a blender or food processor, or rub through a strainer, cool. Whip cream with remaining sugar until thick, then stir in the yogurt. In individual dishes or one large glass bowl, layer apple, crumbs and cream, ending with a layer of crumbs. Chill, serve decorated with whipped cream and chocolate.

Illustrated opposite

OZARK PUDDING

Serves 4

1 egg
½ cup sugar
1 tablespoon all-purpose flour
1½ teaspoons baking powder
½ teaspoon vanilla extract
1 pound cooking apples, peeled,
cored and chopped
⅔ cup chopped walnuts
½ cup heavy cream, whipped

Beat the egg with an electric mixer, then gradually add the sugar and continue beating for about 3 minutes until the sugar is dissolved and the mixture is thick and pale. Blend in the flour, baking powder and vanilla then stir in the apples and walnuts.

Pour the batter into a greased 9-inch pie dish or shallow 5-cup baking dish. Bake in a preheated oven, 350°F, for 25-30 minutes until well browned on top. Set the pudding aside and let cool completely.

To serve, spoon into small glass bowls, layering a little whipped cream in the middle. Top with an extra dollop of whipped cream, and serve.

APPLE ROULADE

Serves 4-6

1 pound tart eating apples peeled,
cored and sliced
grated rind and juice of 1 lemon
3 tablespoons confectioners' sugar
½ cup finely ground almonds
4 eggs, separated
¾ pint raspberries

Place apples in a saucepan with lemon rind, juice and 2 tablespoons of the confectioners' sugar. Cover and cook gently for 15 minutes until soft. Purée them in a blender or food processor, or rub through a strainer. Place in a bowl, stir in the ground almonds, let cool completely before beating the egg yolks into the applesauce. Whisk the egg whites until stiff, fold lightly into the applesauce.

Line a 13 x 9-inch jelly roll pan with oiled waxed paper. Spread apple mixture in the pan. Bake in a preheated oven, 400°F, for about 10-15 minutes, until firm and beginning to brown.

Dust a sheet of waxed paper with the remaining confectioners' sugar. Invert the roulade on the prepared paper, peel off the lining paper. Spread the raspberries over the roulade to within 1 inch of the edges. Lift up the paper to roll up the roulade. Lift carefully on to a dish; serve hot or cold.

CALVADOS APPLES

Serves 4

½ **cup sugar**
1¼ **cups water**
6 **eating apples, peeled and quartered**
3 **tablespoons Calvados or applejack**

CARAMEL:

6 **tablespoons sugar**
3 **tablespoons water**

Place the ½ cup sugar and water in a saucepan and heat gently, stirring until dissolved. Bring to a boil, then simmer for 5 minutes. Add the apples to the syrup, cover and simmer gently for 15-20 minutes until the apples look clear. Let cool in the syrup, then transfer the apples to a glass serving dish.

Boil the syrup rapidly until reduced by about half, then add the Calvados or applejack. Pour over the apples. Let cool.

To make the caramel, place the sugar and water in a pan and heat gently, stirring, until dissolved, then boil rapidly until golden brown. Pour onto an oiled baking sheet and leave to harden. When set, crack the caramel into pieces and sprinkle over the apples. Serve immediately.

PLUM & APPLE MOLD

Serves 4

½ **stick butter**
2 **tablespoons cold water**
½ **pound plums, pitted**
½ **pound tart eating apples, peeled,
cored and thinly sliced**
sugar, to taste
2 **eggs, beaten**
1 **envelope unflavored gelatin,
soaked in 2 tablespoons cold water**
⅔ **cup plain yogurt**

Melt the butter in a large saucepan. Stir in the water and add the fruit. Simmer gently, stirring occasionally, until tender. Purée the fruit in a blender or food processor, or rub through a strainer. Return the purée to the pan and add sugar to taste. Continue to cook over a low heat, stirring constantly, until the purée has thickened.

Remove the pan from the heat and stir in the eggs. Return the pan to the heat and stir constantly until the mixture thickens. Stir in the gelatin. Set aside to cool.

Stir the yogurt into the mixture. Spoon into a serving bowl or mold and chill for at least 2 hours, or until set. To serve, dip the mold or bowl into hot water for 10 seconds and then invert onto a serving plate.

TOFFEE APPLE CHEESECAKE

Serves 8-10

BASE:

¾ stick butter or margarine

1 tablespoon sugar

1½ cups vanilla wafer crumbs

FILLING:

2 cups small-curd cottage cheese

2 eggs, separated

½ cup sugar

grated rind and juice of ½ lemon

1½ envelopes unflavored gelatin

6 tablespoons apple juice

½ cup heavy cream, whipped

¾ cup unsweetened applesauce

1 teaspoon ground cinnamon

TOPPING:

⅓ cup sugar

3 tablespoons water

½ cup heavy cream

⅔ cup heavy cream, whipped

1 apple, cored and sliced and brushed with

1 tablespoon lemon juice

Melt the butter or margarine in a saucepan. Stir in the sugar and wafer crumbs. Press the crumb mixture onto the bottom of a greased 8-inch deep springform cake tin. Chill.

Beat the small-curd cottage cheese in a large mixing bowl. Beat in the egg yolks, sugar and lemon rind and juice.

Sprinkle the gelatin over the apple juice in a small saucepan and let stand for 3 minutes. Place the saucepan over a low heat, stirring, until the gelatin is dissolved. Beat the gelatin into the cheese mixture. Fold in the heavy cream, applesauce and cinnamon. Refrigerate until the mixture is almost set.

Beat the egg whites until stiff. Fold into the cheese mixture. Spoon the cheesecake mixture into the prepared pan and smooth the top. Chill for 3-4 hours or until the filling is set.

For the topping, place the sugar and water in a small saucepan and stir over a low heat until the sugar is dissolved. Bring to a boil and boil gently until the mixture is a thick golden syrup. Remove from the heat and leave for a few seconds only, to let the bubbles subside. Gradually stir in the heavy cream. Reheat gently to dissolve any solidified caramel. Cool.

Carefully remove the sides of the pan and place the cheesecake on a serving plate. Spread the toffee-flavored cream on top of the cheesecake and decorate around the edge with whipped cream and apple slices.

Illustrated opposite

APPLE NUT VACHERIN

Serves 8

MERINGUE:

4 egg whites
1 cup sugar
1 cup finely ground hazelnuts

FILLING:

4 large cooking apples (*about 1¼ pounds*),
peeled, cored and thinly sliced
½ cup superfine sugar
¼ stick butter
2 teaspoons lemon juice
1¼ cups whipping cream

TO DECORATE:

apple slices
toasted hazelnuts

Mark the underside of each of the three sheets of nonstick waxed paper with a 7-inch circle and place each sheet on a lightly greased baking sheet.

Whisk the egg whites until stiff and gradually whisk in the superfine sugar, a tablespoon at a time, continuing to whisk until thick and glossy. Lightly fold in the ground hazelnuts, using a large metal spoon. Divide the mixture among the three circles and spread out on the paper with a metal spatula.

Cook in a preheated oven, 325°F, for about 35-40 minutes until lightly golden and crisp on the outside. Remove from the oven and let cool. Carefully remove from the paper.

To make the filling, put the sliced apples in a saucepan with the sugar, butter and lemon juice. Cover the pan and cook for 15 minutes until tender. Remove the lid and beat well with a wooden spoon then continue cooking for a further 5-8 minutes until the apples form a thick sauce. Remove from the heat and leave to cool.

About 1 hour before serving, whip the cream until it forms soft peaks and fold two-thirds of the quantity into the applesauce. Place one meringue round on a serving plate and spread with half of the applesauce. Place the second round on top, spread it with the remaining sauce and top with the third round.

Pipe swirls of the remaining cream on top of the meringue and decorate with the apple slices and toasted hazelnuts.

Illustrated on pages 2-3

TOFFEE APPLE ICE CREAM

Serves 6

**1 pound cooking apples, peeled,
cored and coarsely chopped
1 cup water plus 1 tablespoon
¼ stick butter, cut into small pieces
¼ cup sugar
2 egg yolks
1¼ cups heavy cream, whipped**

Put the apples in a saucepan with the 1 table-spoon water, cover, and heat gently until they are very soft. Beat in the butter until smooth and let the applesauce cool.

Put sugar and ⅔ cup of the water into a small heavy-bottom saucepan and stir constantly over a low heat until the sugar dissolves completely. Bring to boil, then leave to bubble until a deep golden brown; remove the pan from the heat immediately. Pour on remaining water and stir until caramel dissolves. Return the pan to the heat and boil until the sauce becomes syrupy and reduces by half.

Meanwhile, beat the egg yolks in a bowl until thick and pale. Continue beating and pour on the hot caramel sauce in a thin stream, beating until cool. Fold the applesauce and whipped cream into the egg mixture, and transfer to a freezer container. Cover and freeze until firm without further beating (it may be kept frozen for up to 6 months).

BLACKBERRY & APPLE ICE CREAM

Serves 8

**2 pounds cooking apples, peeled,
cored and coarsely chopped
2 tablespoons lemon juice
2 tablespoons water
¾ pint blackberries
⅔ cup sugar
1¼ cups plain yogurt, chilled
⅔ cup heavy cream, chilled**

TO DECORATE:

**a few blackberries
apple slices, brushed with lemon juice**

Place the apples in a saucepan with the lemon juice and water, cover and cook gently until the apples soften and begin to form a purée.

Stir in the blackberries and sugar and continue to cook for about 5 minutes until the juice runs out of the blackberries. Rub the mixture through a strainer and pour into a freezer container. Refrigerate for 1 hour.

Stir the yogurt into the chilled mixture. Whip the cream until soft peaks form and fold into the mixture. Freeze until firm, beating twice at hourly intervals. (The ice cream may be frozen for up to 6 months.) Serve in individual glass dishes and decorate with blackberries and apple slices.

APPLE & RED CURRANT SNOW

Serves 4

1½ pounds tart cooking apples, peeled, cored and sliced
4 tablespoons red currant jelly
2 tablespoons lemon juice
⅔ cup plain yogurt
2 egg whites
3 tablespoons sugar
1 tablespoon cold water
½ cup slivered almonds

Place apples in a saucepan with 3 tablespoons of red currant jelly and lemon juice. Cover and cook over low heat, stirring occasionally, for 15 minutes, or until the apples are soft.

Purée apples in a blender or food processor, or rub through a strainer. Let the purée cool, then stir in the yogurt. Whisk the egg whites until stiff then whisk in the sugar and fold into the apple and yogurt mixture. Spoon into one serving bowl or four individual dishes.

Gently heat the remaining red currant jelly in a saucepan with the water until the jelly has dissolved. Add the slivered almonds to the pan. Stir gently until the almonds are glazed. Tip out onto a plate or a piece of foil and let cool. Arrange the glazed almonds on top of the "snow" and serve.

APPLE SHERBET

Serves 4

⅔ cup dry white wine
⅓ cup soft firmly packed brown sugar
a strip of thinly pared lemon rind
2 tablespoons lemon juice
a small piece of fresh ginger, peeled
1 pound cooking apples, peeled, cored and sliced
2 egg whites
small herb leaves such as lemon geranium, to decorate

Put the wine, sugar, lemon rind and juice and ginger into a saucepan and stir over a low heat until the sugar dissolves. Increase the heat and bring to a boil. Add the apple slices, poach them for 8-10 minutes, or until soft. Remove from the heat and let cool.

Discard the lemon rind and ginger and purée the fruit in a blender or food processor, or rub through a strainer. Pour the fruit into a freezer container, cover and freeze for 1 hour.

Beat the egg whites until stiff. Tip the frozen mixture into a chilled bowl and beat it to break down the ice crystals. Fold in the egg whites. Return the mixture to the freezer for 3-4 hours, until firm. To serve, transfer the sherbet to the refrigerator for 30 minutes, scoop out and decorate with the herb leaves.

Illustrated opposite

APPLE LOAF

Makes 1 small loaf

3 cups all-purpose flour
1 tablespoon baking powder
1 stick butter or margarine
½ cup sugar
1 teaspoon apple pie spice
½ teaspoon ground cloves
1 large cooking apple, peeled,
cored and shredded
¼ cup apple cider
1 tablespoon brown sugar

Sift the flour into a bowl with the baking powder. Cut and rub in the fat until mixture resembles fine bread crumbs. Stir in the sugar and spices, then add the apples and mix well. Stir in the apple cider to make a stiff mixture.

Spoon the mixture into a well-greased 9 x 5-inch loaf pan. Sprinkle with the brown sugar and bake in a preheated oven, 375°F, for about 50-55 minutes, or until risen, golden on top and firm to the touch. When cooked, a skewer inserted into the center of the loaf should come out clean. Leave in the pan for a few minutes, before inverting on a wire rack to cool.

Serve warm or cold, cut into thick slices, with butter and clotted cream.

DUTCH APPLE CAKE

Makes an 8-inch round cake

2¼ cups self-rising flour
½ teaspoon salt
1 tablespoon sugar
1 stick butter, diced
½ cup milk
2 Granny Smith apples, peeled,
cored and thinly sliced
TOPPING:
2 tablespoons melted butter
1 teaspoon cinnamon
2 tablespoons sugar

Grease an 8-inch round cake pan and line the base with waxed paper.

Sift the flour, salt and sugar together, and rub in the butter with your fingertips. Make a well in the center and add the milk in a steady stream, stirring with a fork and incorporating the flour. Place the mixture in the prepared pan and pat level, making sure it is pushed well into the edges and against the sides.

Arrange the apples in a circular pattern to cover the top of the cake, pressing the thin edges into the dough. Brush with melted butter, sprinkle with the cinnamon and sugar, and bake in a preheated oven, 350°F, for 55 minutes. This cake is best served warm, cut into wedges and buttered.

CARROT & APPLE CAKE

Makes 16-20 pieces

⅔ **cup packed soft brown sugar**
2 eggs, beaten
⅔ **cup corn oil**
¾ **cup self-rising flour**
1 cup whole wheat flour
2 teaspoons baking powder
½ **teaspoon baking soda**
1 teaspoon apple pie spice
½ **teaspoon ground ginger**
½ **teaspoon ground nutmeg**
1½ **cups grated carrot**
1 eating apple, peeled, cored and grated
⅓ **cup golden raisins**
1 tablespoon apple juice
1 package (*3 ounces*) cream cheese, softened
2 tablespoons plain yogurt
½ **cup chopped nuts**

Beat sugar and eggs together until frothy. Gradually beat in the oil. Combine the dry ingredients, stir into the egg mixture with the carrot, apple and golden raisins. Add apple juice to give consistency of thick batter. Pour into a greased, base-lined 8-inch square cake pan. Bake in a preheated oven, 350°F, for 40-50 minutes or until firm and risen. Cool on a wire rack. Beat together the cream cheese and yogurt. Drizzle over the cake, sprinkle with nuts and cut into squares.

CHOCOLATE & APPLE CAKE

Makes an 8-inch square cake

1 cup all-purpose flour
1 teaspoon apple pie spice
1 teaspoon baking powder
½ **teaspoon baking soda**
1 cup whole wheat flour
1 stick butter
1 cup firmly packed soft brown sugar
2 eggs, beaten
⅔ **cup dried currants**
⅔ **cup raisins or golden raisins**
½ **cup semisweet or milk chocolate chips**
grated rind of 1 small orange
1 cooking apple, peeled and coarsely grated
2 tablespoons dark brown sugar

Sift all-purpose flour, spice, baking powder and soda into a bowl, add whole wheat flour. Cream fat and sugar in a bowl until pale and fluffy. Add eggs, one at a time, adding a little flour after each. Fold in remaining flour then the rest of the ingredients except the dark brown sugar. Add 1 tablespoon water if mixture seems dry. Spoon into a greased and lined 8-inch square cake pan. Level, sprinkle with dark brown sugar. Bake in a preheated oven, 350°F, for about 45 minutes or until firm to the touch and golden brown. Cool in the pan for 5 minutes then turn out on to a wire rack. Store in an airtight container when cold – best left 48 hours before cutting.

APPLESAUCE CAKE

Makes 9 squares

1 cup raisins
2 cups all-purpose flour
2 teaspoons baking soda
½ teaspoon ground nutmeg
¼ teaspoon ground cloves
½ teaspoon ground cinnamon
1 stick butter
1 cup firmly packed soft brown sugar
1 egg
½ teaspoon vanilla extract
1½ cups unsweetened applesauce
1 cup chopped walnuts or pecans
chopped walnuts or pecans,
to decorate (*optional*)

FROSTING:

1 package (*8 ounces*) cream cheese, softened
¼ cup firmly packed dark brown sugar
¼ teaspoon grated orange rind
¼ teaspoon vanilla extract
2 teaspoons light cream or milk

Soak the raisins in enough hot water to cover them for 15 minutes, then drain, discarding the soaking water.

Sift the all-purpose flour, baking soda and spices together and set aside.

Beat the butter with brown sugar until well creamed and the sugar has dissolved. Beat in the egg and vanilla, then stir in the applesauce and chopped nuts. Add the dry ingredients to the creamed mixture in three batches, folding well to combine after each addition.

Pour the cake into a well-greased 9-inch square, or 7½ x 11-inch rectangular, baking pan. Bake in a preheated oven, 350°F, for about 50 minutes, or until a skewer inserted in the center comes out clean. Cool in the baking pan on a wire rack.

Beat all the frosting ingredients together until smooth and well blended. Spread the frosting over the top of the cooled cake. Decorate with chopped walnuts or pecans, if desired. Cut into squares to serve.

Illustrated opposite

APPLE CHEESECAKES

Makes 12

½ pound apples, cored and coarsely
chopped (*not peeled*)
4-5 tablespoons water
thinly pared rind of ½ lemon
2-3 whole cloves
½ stick cinnamon,
or pinch of ground cinnamon
1-2 tablespoons sugar
¼ cup butter
⅓ cup cake crumbs or fresh bread crumbs
2 egg yolks, or 1 whole egg, beaten
sugar, for sprinkling

DOUGH:
1 cup all-purpose flour
pinch of salt
½ stick butter
1 tablespoon sugar
1 egg yolk

To make the dough, sift the flour and salt into a mixing bowl. Cut the butter into the flour and rub in until the mixture resembles bread crumbs. Stir in the superfine sugar, then stir in the egg yolk to bind to a firm dough, adding a little cold water if necessary.

Knead lightly until smooth but do not overwork the dough. Leave to rest in the refrigerator or a cool place for at least 30 minutes before rolling out.

Place the apples, water, lemon rind, cloves, cinnamon and sugar in a saucepan. Cover and cook until softened. Remove the lid and continue cooking into a thick pulp, stirring frequently so it does not stick. Remove the cinnamon stick, if using.

Purée the apples in a blender or food processor, or rub through a strainer, and return to the rinsed pan over a gentle heat. Add the butter and when melted remove the pan from the heat. Cool slightly, then stir in the cake crumbs or fresh bread crumbs and egg. Leave until cold.

Roll out the dough thinly and line 12 small patty pans. Prick the bottom of each and three-quarters fill with the apple mixture. Bake in a preheated oven, 400°F, for 20 minutes, or until the dough is crisp and the filling set. Remove from the pans and cool on a wire rack. When cold, sprinkle generously with sugar, and serve.

LITTLE MARZIPAN & APPLE PIES

Makes 12

milk, for brushing
1 tablespoon soft brown sugar (*optional*)

FILLING:

1 large cooking apple, peeled,
cored and coarsely chopped
3 ounces ready-made marzipan,
cut into ¼ inch (*about ½ cup*) cubes

DOUGH:

1 cup all-purpose flour
1 cup whole wheat flour
pinch of salt
1 stick margarine, frozen
3-4 tablespoons water

To make the dough, put both the flours and the salt into a large bowl. Grate the frozen margarine straight into the flours, dipping it into the bowl now and again to free the flakes of margarine. Distribute the margarine gently through the flour, using a round-bladed knife, then add the water as necessary. Mix to a fairly firm dough then put the dough into a plastic bag and chill in the refrigerator for 1 hour if possible.

For the filling, mix the chopped apple and marzipan cubes together in a bowl.

Roll out the dough quite thinly on a lightly floured surface. Cut out twelve rounds using a 3-inch fluted cutter, and twelve rounds using a 2-inch fluted cutter. Line twelve small tart pans with the larger rounds and spoon the apple and marzipan filling into them, packing it in well.

Brush both sides of the remaining rounds with milk and lay them on top of the tarts in the pan. Press the edges together to seal and sprinkle each one with a little brown sugar, if you like.

Bake near the top of a preheated oven, 425°F, for 15-20 minutes until golden brown. Remove carefully from the pans and let cool slightly on a wire rack. Serve warm or cold.

DATE & APPLE CRUNCHIES

Makes 16

1 stick butter or margarine
⅔ cup firmly packed soft brown sugar
3 tablespoons light corn syrup
1½ cups rolled oats
1 cup whole wheat flour
1 teaspoon baking powder
⅔ cup chopped dates
1½ cups finely chopped peeled apples

Melt the butter with the sugar and syrup in a saucepan over a gentle heat. Stir well and do not let boil. Set aside to cool slightly. Mix together the rolled oats, flour and baking powder. Stir in the cooled liquid ingredients and mix very thoroughly.

Mix the chopped dates with the apples. Add to the oat mixture and mix until well distributed. Spoon the mixture into an 8-inch square cake pan and press down firmly.

Bake in a preheated oven, 350°F, for 30-35 minutes until firm and golden. Remove from oven, cut into squares. Let cool, remove from the pan and cool on a wire rack. Store in an airtight container.

HOT APPLE MUFFINS

Makes 24

2 cups all-purpose flour
1 teaspoon salt
1 tablespoon baking powder
¼ cup sugar
½ teaspoon ground ginger
½ teaspoon apple pie spice
2 eggs, beaten
⅔ cup milk
¼ cup melted butter
1½ cups finely chopped peeled apples

Grease 24 x 2-inch muffin pans. Sift the flour, salt and baking powder into a mixing bowl. Stir in the sugar and spices. In a small bowl beat the eggs with the milk and mix in the melted butter. Stir the liquid quickly into the flour mixture. Speed is essential once the liquid is added to the baking powder, so do not beat the mixture since the mixture should be lumpy. Fold in the chopped apples. Spoon the mixture into the greased muffin pans so they are one-third full.

Bake in a preheated oven, 425°F, for 15-20 minutes or until well risen and golden brown. Remove from the pans and serve hot, split and buttered.

Illustrated opposite

SPICED APPLE DRINK

Makes 2½ quarts

1 pound apples
2½ quarts cold water
1 cup sugar
1 tablespoon ground ginger
1 tablespoon ground cinnamon
½ tablespoon whole cloves
½ tablespoon allspice

Wash the apples and grate them coarsely into a clean 3 quart wide-necked container, such as a plastic pail or bowl. Add the apple cores and the cold water. Put in a cool place for 1 week and stir once a day.

Add the sugar and spices. Stir the liquid until the sugar has dissolved. Leave to stand for 1 day more, then strain the liquid through cheesecloth. Siphon or pour the liquid into clean bottles.

Lightly cork the bottles and leave them in a cool place for 1 week before drinking.

MULLED APPLE JUICE

Makes 4 cups

1 pound cooking apples, peeled,
cored and sliced
2½ cups water
finely grated rind and juice of 2 oranges
6 tablespoons honey
6 whole cloves, or large pinch of ground cloves
1 cinnamon stick, or pinch of ground cinnamon
1 teaspoon ground nutmeg
pinch of ground ginger
2 tablespoons rum or brandy

TO DECORATE:

whole cloves

apple slices

Put all the ingredients, except the rum or brandy, in a saucepan. Bring to a boil, then lower the heat, cover the pan and simmer for about 10 minutes until the apples are reduced to a pulp.

Transfer to a blender or food processor and blend until the apples are smooth, but the whole spices, if used, are still in pieces.

Strain the juice, stir in the rum or brandy and serve hot, decorated with whole cloves and slices of apple.

Illustrated on pages 2-3

BLACKBERRY & APPLE JAM

Makes about 7 pounds

2 pounds cooking apples, peeled, cored
and keep trimmings
1¼ cups water
3 pints blackberries
8 cups sugar
½ cup lemon juice

Boil apple trimmings in a saucepan with water for 15 minutes, or until most of the water has evaporated. Put apples, blackberries and 1 cup of sugar in a large pan. Press apple trimmings through a fine strainer to extract pulp and pectin, add this to the fruit. Heat gently until juice runs from blackberries, cook for 5-10 minutes, or until apples are soft.

Add remaining sugar to pan, stir over a gentle heat until dissolved. Add lemon juice. Bring to a boil, boiling hard until setting point is reached: put a little jam on a cold saucer and let cool. Setting point is reached if a skin forms on the surface and wrinkles when gently pushed with one finger. Alternatively, use a candy thermometer – this should register 220°F when setting point is reached.

Pour the hot jam in to warmed pots, cover with small rounds of waxed paper. Cool. Cover with airtight lids and store, for 6-9 months. U.S.D.A. suggests processing jelly in a water-bath canner jar for at least 5 minutes.

APPLE MINCEMEAT

Makes about 6 pounds

1 pound cooking apples, peeled,
cored and grated (*about 3½ cups*)
1⅓ cups cut dried candied citrus peel
2½ cups dried currants
2½ cups golden raisins
2½ cups raisins
1½ sticks chilled butter, grated
2 cups granulated or firmly packed
soft brown sugar
1 cup chopped almonds
1½ teaspoons ground apple pie spice
1 teaspoon ground nutmeg
grated rind and juice of 1 lemon
⅔ cup brandy or rum

Place all the ingredients, except the brandy or rum, in a large bowl and mix well. Cover and leave for 24 hours, then add the spirit and mix again. Pack the mincemeat into sterilized jars and cover.

If the mincemeat is to be kept for more than a few weeks, seal the jars with an airtight cover – glass or plastic-coated lids are suitable, or corks which have been soaked in boiling water for 15 minutes to sterilize them. U.S.D.A. suggests processing jelly in a water-bath canner jar for at least 5 minutes.

APPLE & HORSERADISH SAUCE

Makes about 2 cups

1 pound cooking apples, coarsely chopped
2 tablespoons water
2 whole cloves
¼ cup sugar
¼ stick butter
1 teaspoon lemon juice
2 tablespoons grated horseradish
or bottled horseradish sauce

Place the chopped apples in a saucepan with the water, cloves and sugar. Simmer until tender, then beat until smooth. Purée in a blender or food processor, or rub through a strainer. Stir in the butter, lemon juice and horseradish and reheat gently. Serve the sauce with fish or meat. Store for up to 3 days in the refrigerator.

APPLE CHUTNEY

Makes about 6 pounds

3 pounds cooking apples, peeled,
cored and chopped
3 pounds onions, chopped
2 cups raisins
2 ounces fresh ginger, minced
(*about ¼ cup*)
1 sweet green pepper, cored,
seeded and chopped
1 tablespoon mustard powder
1 tablespoon ground coriander
3 garlic cloves, crushed
4 cups firmly packed dark brown sugar
2½ cups vinegar

Put all the ingredients together in a large saucepan and mix well. Bring slowly to a boil, stirring occasionally, then reduce the heat and cover the pan. Leave the chutney to simmer for about 2 hours, or until the mixture is thick. Stir the mixture often to prevent it sticking to the pan.

Spoon the chutney into clean, warmed pots and cover with small rounds of waxed paper, waxed sides down. Top immediately with airtight lids. Store for a few weeks before sampling; the chutney can be kept for up to 6 months. U.S.D.A. suggests processing jelly in a water-bath canner jar for at least 5 minutes.

Illustrated opposite

CHUNKY APPLE SAUCE

Makes about 1½ cups

½ stick butter
1 large Spanish onion, finely diced
8 fresh sage leaves, chopped,
or 2 teaspoons dried
2 tablespoons soft brown sugar
1 pound eating apples, peeled,
cored and sliced
salt and freshly ground black pepper

Melt the butter in a saucepan and gently sauté the onion. Add the sage and salt and pepper, and cook until the onion is soft and transparent, stirring occasionally.

Sprinkle over the brown sugar, increase the heat and stir in the sliced apples. Cook for 7-10 minutes, turning the mixture over occasionally with a wooden spoon, but taking care not to break the apple slices.

As soon as the apples are soft, but not mushy, remove from the heat. The sauce makes an ideal accompaniment to serve with duck, pork or goose.

SPICED APPLE SLICES

Makes about 4 pounds

2 cups sugar
2½ cups white vinegar
1 teaspoon salt
½ cup water
6-inch cinnamon stick
2 teaspoons whole cloves
few drops red food coloring
3 pounds eating apples, peeled,
cored and thickly sliced

Put the sugar and white vinegar into a saucepan with the salt and water. Tie the spices in a cheesecloth of muslin and hang them in the pan. Stir over a low heat until the sugar has dissolved. Add a little food coloring and stir to color evenly.

Drop the apple slices into the hot spiced syrup and cook gently until they are tender but still keep their shape. Skim out the slices and pack them into warm preserving jars. Then heat the syrup to boiling point and pour into the jars, covering the apple slices. Cover tightly.

These are delicious served with cold lamb, ham and pork, or with cold goose or duck.

APPLE & APRICOT STUFFING

Sufficient for a 3-pound roasting chicken

**1 large cooking apple, peeled,
cored and finely chopped
⅔ cup chopped dried apricots
2 cups fresh bread crumbs
1 onion, finely chopped
1 teaspoon dried thyme
1 teaspoon dried sage
¼ cup brandy or dry sherry
2 tablespoons orange juice
salt and freshly ground black pepper**

Mix the chopped apple and apricots with the fresh bread crumbs. Add the chopped onion, dried herbs, brandy or dry sherry and orange juice. Season and mix well to make a moist stuffing for roast chicken.

APPLE & RAISIN STUFFING

Sufficient for 3-pound roasting chicken

**½ stick butter
1 onion, finely chopped
8 fresh sage leaves, chopped,
or 2 teaspoons dried
2 eating apples, peeled, cored and diced
¼ cup long-grain rice, cooked and drained
⅓ cup raisins
1 egg yolk, lightly beaten
salt and freshly ground black pepper**

Melt the butter in a saucepan and gently cook the onion for about 4 minutes, until soft and transparent. Increase the heat, add the sage and diced apples, and toss over the heat for 6-7 minutes, until the apples soften but do not entirely lose their shape.

Add the rice, raisins and salt and pepper, stirring well. Remove from the heat and cool slightly. Beat in the egg yolk to bind all the ingredients together. Use as a stuffing for roast chicken or serve with duck, goose or pork.

THE
APPLE
INDEX